Everything You Need
To Know About
Mystery Shopping

Everything You Need To Know About Mystery Shopping

K. A. Daugherty

To order additional copies of this book, contact:
Xlibris Corporation
1-888-795-4274
www.Xlibris.com
Orders@Xlibris.com
60130

Table of Contents

Foreword

IT WAS THE summer of my junior year in high school when I first heard about mystery shopping. I was trying to save up some money by working at my part-time retail job at a department store in the mall. One afternoon a co-worker of mine was visibly upset, and mentioned she'd just been "shopped." Apparently she got a bad report and just had a long and unpleasant conversation with our store manager.

I thought, "Hmmm . . . she was shopped. Well, sure. We work in a department store." She explained to me that a mystery shopper had been hired to report on the customer service of the store and to make sure she "did everything right." This certainly seemed strange to me, but I went along with it. Over the course of that summer, our store was shopped several more times. Each salesperson got different ratings of course, some good and some bad.

In my young mind, I naively believed that we certainly would know who the mystery shopper was because she would be wearing a big floppy hat, an obviously fake wig, giant sunglasses, and possibly even a trench coat. But despite the fantasy I had concocted in my head of this mystery shopper, with each customer that walked in, there was always that thought in the back of my head that perhaps that person is *the one*. Eventually all the customers started looking suspicious to us. By the end of the summer, everyone working at the store was performing at their best and servicing each and every customer the way the company taught us to in training sessions.

And that is exactly the reason why so many companies hire mystery shoppers. Companies want to find out where their stores, restaurants, movie theaters, and so forth are failing their patrons. Is the store's customer service problem confined to one employee? Is it a management problem? Is there one area in particular that their patrons are complaining about, where perhaps some extra training would be useful? The co-worker who had received the bad report had always presented a professional and friendly image, and in my eyes she was a great employee. Yet somewhere between the main offices of the company, and down through the ranks of regional and store management, there were some discrepancies between what the definition of a "good" employee exactly was. Perhaps a friendly greeting was provided to the customer within five minutes rather than the corporate requirement of two minutes. Or perhaps additional merchandise wasn't suggested when she was ringing up her customer. And yet despite the fact that the customer service issues may have appeared to be with her, she may have been performing her duties exactly as she was trained to do. The problem may have actually been that the training sessions or management were failing to show the sales staff what was expected of them. So mystery shopping not only helps the company to determine how well the front team members are performing, but it shows them where training and management may be under-performing as well.

After college, I got out of the retail industry. As so many others do, I spent four long, hard years working for a diploma so I could spend my days sitting in the dreary confines of a cubicle, getting the same paycheck every two weeks regardless of how hard I did or did not work. I went to restaurants for lunch and dinner, and I often complained about the poor service to my friends and family. I went to shopping malls and complained about the long lines and lack of attention I received from the salespeople. I noticed how dirty some stores were, and how unpleasant and unwelcoming the atmosphere was.

But as most people do, I continued on with my life, occasionally mumbling under my breath quietly about poor service or a bad salesperson, with my blood pressure slightly higher than it probably should have been after some shopping trips. But what can you do? After all, this is just the way the world is now. Customer service is mostly gone, and stores and restaurants for the most part don't care. Right?

Wrong.

As the years went by, I grew tired of my desk job, as well as the lack of raises and the doldrums that come with doing the same old thing every day. I wanted to mix things up a bit. And I wanted to make some extra money. So I began an earnest search looking for a part-time job in the evenings or on weekends to supplement my income. My only requirements were that my new job did not interfere with my current job, and that it was exciting and flexible. I didn't start out wanting to be a mystery shopper. And honestly, when I stumbled upon mystery shopping in my search for part-time work, I was very wary. Even having my retail background and having worked in a store that had been hit by mystery shoppers repeatedly, it didn't sound like real work.

But curiosity got the best of me, so I looked into it a little more. I proceeded cautiously, as I was anxious to do something else, anything else at all. And the idea that by shopping and reporting back to stores on my experiences I could actually improve customer service really appealed to me. Not only would my concerns be listened to, but the stores were actually asking for my feedback and were paying me for it. Finally, I could actually do something about all that under-my-breath complaining I'd been doing over the years!

So I registered with a few companies, did my first shop assignment about a week later, and the rest is history. I make it sound easy, but there was quite a learning curve. My goals in writing this book are to help you decide if mystery shopping is the right job for you, define which rumors floating around are fact or fiction, and lead you on the path to getting started with a profitable career as a mystery shopper.

Chapter 1

The History of Mystery Shopping

THERE ARE A wide variety of companies that use mystery shoppers. They include banks, gas stations, retail stores, restaurants, movie theaters, fitness centers, car dealerships, apartment complexes, and many others. These companies hire mystery shoppers for so many reasons. Some companies want to ensure customer satisfaction, while others want to determine areas where their staff's sales techniques are lacking. Mystery shopping may be used to verify satisfaction with the product or service purchased, or to gauge the store's impression on its customers for areas such as cleanliness, atmosphere, and so forth. These are all important factors to a store's viability and profitability. For this reason, companies take the results of a mystery shopper's report very seriously. But how did this all begin?

Mystery shopping originally started back in the 1940s, when employee theft at banks was a widespread problem. Banks hired private investigators to pose as customers in the banks and catch crooked employees in the act. This covert type of mystery shopping involving the policing of employees moved in to retail stores shortly thereafter, and eventually evolved into the type of shopping we know today. While the main concentration of mystery shopping today is on improving customer satisfaction and sales techniques, the focus earlier in its history was aimed largely on monitoring employees. In most cases today, companies are using mystery shoppers to improve their stores, rather than to build a case to fire bad employees.

In the 1970s and 1980s, a handful of mystery shopping companies became more prevalent in the media. With this publicity, mystery shopping grew in popularity. More companies, and more *types* of companies, became aware of the benefits mystery shopping could bring to their companies. Because of the incredible growth in demand from companies wanting to use mystery shoppers during this time period, there was a tremendous increase in the number of mystery shoppers.

In the 1990s, the internet became more mainstream, causing a major shift in how mystery shopping was conducted. Prior to the 90s, mystery shoppers typically had to mail in their questionnaires, receipts and any undercover audio or video tapes. With the advent of the internet, however, all paperwork could be transmitted electronically, greatly speeding up the paperwork aspect of mystery shopping. However, as with most information conveyed electronically, companies became aware of the growing need to verify the accuracy of the information they were receiving, and now required additional verification to ensure the shops were done correctly. Today, receipts submitted electronically may now be verified by the companies to rule out fraudulent activity. The times logged by a shopper may now be verified by in-store cameras. Any information that was found to be fraudulent or inaccurate could result in that shop being invalidated and the mystery shopper not being paid for it. In addition, the mystery shopper's rating with that mystery shopping provider likely would decrease and hurt the chance of that shopper getting future shops with that company.

The internet also allowed for an easier way to connect mystery shopping providers with shoppers. Providers could now screen and accept new applicants via the internet, greatly reducing the time and effort needed to get new shoppers signed up. In addition, shoppers now had access at their fingertips to search for additional mystery shopping companies and increase their earning potential. Today, it is not uncommon for shoppers to now be signed up and active with anywhere from 10-30 or more providers at a time. These factors played into a large increase in the number of mystery shoppers.

Mystery shoppers also now had the ease and speed of searching for and applying for shop assignments online. When new jobs are posted online, all shoppers that fit the profile of that shop assignment are automatically sent an email notice. Some shops are posted online as self-assign, meaning these shops are taken by the first person who gets to them. This creates a very fast turnaround time on jobs being assigned. In fact, many shops are now assigned to shoppers within hours of being offered online.

Today, there are thousands of companies who use mystery shoppers regularly, and several hundred mystery shopping providers you can sign up to work with. Mystery shoppers are in high demand worldwide, with the industry income closing in on $1.5 billion annually as of the publication of this book. With this demand for mystery shoppers also comes the vulnerability for scams, which have been made more public in recent years. The Mystery Shopper Providers Association provides legitimacy to providers worldwide, aiding mystery shoppers in determining the scams from the legitimate providers.

Despite the scams, however, mystery shopping proves to be a viable alternative to a traditional part-time job, and for some even a full-time job.

Chapter 2

Can You Be A Mystery Shopper?
(And should you?)

MYSTERY SHOPPING MAY sound like a fun side job. Who doesn't want to make money shopping? There are thousands of mystery shoppers worldwide who are very satisfied with their job. And yet countless others try it out and decide it's not for them. Before you jump into the job, you should be aware that this is a serious and legitimate job. The glamorous, almost spy-like job title leads many potential mystery shoppers to believe that the job requires you to walk around a shopping mall at your leisure, visiting all of your favorite stores, and making notes on your experiences and opinions about salespeople. This is not true. There are pre-qualifications, requirements, and real work that is required for each shop assignment. Yet the skill set required to be a mystery shopper is fairly minimal. And likewise, the pay for the large majority (but not all) of the shop assignments is fairly comparable to most non-skilled part-time jobs.

The Good . . .

Shoppers who get into this job and stick with it tend to do it for more than the just the money or the mystique, although those are certainly benefits as well. Mystery shoppers have a legitimate desire to help companies improve the overall shopping experience of their customers. They feel that their efforts will actually make a difference, and they enjoy getting paid for companies to really listen to their opinions and experiences.

They may enjoy the covert, spy-like mentality of the job. There may be a small part in each of us that wants to play James Bond. Mystery shopping allows this hidden fantasy to play out, but with much less risk. We certainly won't be shot at or chased down a street by a helicopter in a typical shop. Yet we still enjoy the hidden knowledge that we will report back on everything we experience while in the store, and there is a subtle thrill to this. You have a secret when you walk into that store, and in that secret comes a sense of power.

Mystery shopping also allows the pay of a typical part-time job with the convenience of a very flexible schedule. With this job, you aren't required to work every Wednesday from 4-8pm, or a 12-hour shift on Saturday. You can sneak in a quick mystery shop assignment on your lunch break from your normal 9-5 job, and you may even get a free lunch out of it. Stay-at-home parents can bring their children on many shop assignments, which makes this an attractive way to earn income without the need for childcare. Retirees have found that mystery shopping is a great way to supplement their income and still enjoy the freedom retirement brings them. College students use mystery shopping as a means to get extra spending money while still having plenty of time for their studies. So many different types of lifestyles make use of the flexibility a job like mystery shopping offers them.

With so many different types of shops to choose from, you have the option of only working assignments that sound enjoyable to you. For instance, if you enjoy going to movies, you may want to specialize in doing movie theater trailer checks. If you regularly eat out, there are so many restaurant shops available that will provide a stipend for your food bill, as well as pay for your time. There are even shops to test drive new cars, view model homes, and try out new gyms. However you enjoy spending your time, there are surely shops that you will enjoy spending your time on.

The Bad . . . And the Ugly.

As I mentioned, mystery shopping is a real job. And with any real job, there is real work to be done. Your shop assignment will come with requirements that must be met if you are to get paid for the assignment. The company hiring you typically has a certain area or issue they want to monitor. For instance, a retail store may want to ensure employees working a certain shift are up-selling and cross-selling properly, and are properly monitoring fitting rooms. So your assignment may be to take a low-dollar item into a fitting room and then attempt to purchase that item. You may be asked to report on how the employee tried to up-sell you to a higher dollar item, or to entice you to purchase additional items. The store may be interested in noting if you received additional attention from the salesperson while you were actually in the fitting room.

For a restaurant shop, the restaurant may be interested in how the kitchen staff is performing. So you may be asked to order certain menu items to ensure the taste and temperature of the food is up to par, and that the kitchen's timing is satisfactory.

With each assignment you will have certain tasks you need to complete, and these tasks will be based on areas the company or store needs to monitor. Failure to follow the shop assignment requirements precisely will result in a pay deduction, or may invalidate your shop entirely – resulting in no payment at all for that shop. As a mystery shopper, you do not have carte blanche to walk into the store of your choice, peruse whatever items interest you at your leisure, purchase whatever you like, and then be reimbursed for your purchase and time. Unfortunately the job doesn't quite work like this. Many new shoppers get into the business thinking they will have the freedom to shop where the like and get paid for it, but this is not the case.

Once you've left the location of the shop, be it a store or restaurant or so on, your job isn't over. A shop requirement typically requires you to file your report and provide receipts as necessary to validate your shop, and this paperwork typically needs to be completed within 12-24 hours of your visit. Some reports are multiple choice type questions, others are short essay. At minimum, you typically need to note the names of all staff that helped you, as well as the time you entered and left the location. Some shops require much more detail than this. For instance, on some shops, you may be asked to review each and every display in the store and ensure it was set up properly. For this, you would be asked to memorize how the displays are supposed to look, and then keep track of what was wrong with each display in the store. This can get challenging since you can't take the paperwork into the store with you and you may have five, ten, or more displays to memorize.

And then comes the not-so-small matter of pay. Payment for completing your shop assignment in most cases is not immediate. Your paperwork will need to be reviewed and approved, and then your payment will be processed. This typically takes anywhere from 30-60 days on average. However, some providers will pay you within a week or so if you accept payment through a PayPal account. If you're looking for quick money, this job is generally not for you. Although once you get into the job and are completing a steady number of assignments each month, you will begin to see a steady flow of income from this job.

Further, on many shop assignments you will be asked to make a purchase out of your own pocket. Typically this is a small purchase (under $10 usually). You may be permitted to return the item, or you may be required to return or keep the item you purchased. In many cases, the cost of an unreturned purchase will be reimbursed to you within that 30-60 day time frame.

Shop pay is not glamorous by any means. Pay varies greatly by your location, but on average shops typically pay anywhere from $5-40 per shop. The more intensive shop assignments with more detailed reporting required typically pay more, but this is not always the case. Many shoppers have signed up to do a "quick" $5 shop only to be dismayed by having to complete a 60-question report. A shopper who regularly handles a few shops per week can probably reasonably average about $250-450/month in income. This is decent pay considering the flexibility and low-stress level of the job. However, many new shoppers enter the field believing they will get rich with this job, and unfortunately that is not the case.

There are a handful of mystery shoppers who have turned this into a full-time job and make several thousand dollars per month. These shoppers work the equivalent of full-time hours and have long-standing and established relationships with their providers and schedulers, who regularly provide them with a steady stream of work. Full-time mystery shoppers are few and far between. The bottom line is that mystery shopping is great part-time money if you put time into it, but very few people use mystery shopping as their full-time profession.

Do You Have What It Takes?

As you can probably tell, mystery shopping is not for everyone. There is a certain skill set mystery shoppers need to thrive at this job. First and foremost, shoppers need to be very detail-oriented. You will need to be able to read and understand your shop requirements, and follow all the intricate details the shop assignment requires of you. If you are asked to analyze a display and report back on if the display was set up correctly, you cannot bring a photo of the properly-set-up display with you to the shop. You would need to memorize the display photo in your head, and then make mental notes of the display once you are in the shop. (Or otherwise snap an incognito photo of the display, but only if you're sure this can be done without anyone seeing.) You will be asked to remember the names of every sales staff you encounter, as well as keep tabs on conversations you have with each of them. You will need to make note of the times you entered and left the store, and possibly other times – such as how long you stood in line at the check-out, how long it took after you entered the store before you were greeted, and so on. You are required to remember all of this WITHOUT the use of any notes by you. Everything will need to be stored in your head until you get back into the privacy of your car to take notes on your shop. Failure to remember these details will result in invalidation of the shop or lowered pay. So you can see that both attention to detail and a good memory are major requirements of the job.

Companies are hiring you as their eyes and ears in the store, on their behalf. They want you to report on the cleanliness of the facility, friendliness and knowledge of the staff, how you viewed their product, and so forth. Your report should be impartial and fair. If you accept a shop for a fast food restaurant you already hate from past experience, your opinion going into the shop will already be tainted. If you feel you cannot be impartial, skip over that shop assignment. Remember, your opinion and impartiality are highly valued by the company, and information you provide to the company may have far-reaching ramifications. It may be used to help train new employees or to aid in continued training on existing employees.

Shop assignments are typically required to be done in a certain time frame. For instance, a car dealership may want to ensure customers visiting on Saturday afternoons are receiving the attention they need during peak business hours and are able to test drive cars in a reasonable time frame. So this shop assignment may require you to shop between 2 and 5pm on Saturday afternoon. Doing this shop at 10am on Saturday would be of little use to the company. A restaurant may want to ensure their weekday morning staff is friendly and prompt, so that shop may require you to visit the location between 7 and 9am any day between Monday and Friday. Typically there is a little flexibility on when the shop is actually completed, but there will be requirements the company sets forth so its objectives in paying for the shop are met. If you are unable to follow the time requirements set forth, do not accept that particular shop assignment.

In addition, there is a strict time frame in which you must complete your shop reports, typically within 12-24 hours of visiting the site. This will be verified by the receipts you are required to provide with your paperwork. So to be a successful mystery shopper, you should be reliable and responsible, as well as able to meet deadlines.

While most of the reports have some multiple choice or yes/no questions, even these types of questionnaires typically have some essay responses to them. For instance, a question may read "Was the waiter knowledgeable of the menu items? If yes, provide an example of how they showed knowledge. If no, explain why." In addition to being accurate for content, your report should be free of grammatical and spelling errors. If writing is truly something you avoid at all costs, mystery shopping is not for you.

Am I What They Want?

OK, so all of this sounds great to you, and you're ready to sign up. How do you get started? Not so fast . . . Mystery shopping providers are typically fairly open about who they accept as shoppers. With so many different companies needing shoppers, each with their own unique clientèle, providers look for shoppers young and old, with higher and lower income levels, with different education backgrounds, and so forth. There are times, however, when one company has too many shoppers in one location, or too many shoppers of a certain age group, and so on. So, while unlikely, it is possible that you will be turned down as a shopper for a certain provider based purely on your personal attributes as a shopper. With so many providers out there, being passed over by one provider is not something to worry about or to take personally. Simply move on and apply with the next provider.

Chapter 3

Let's Get Started!
What You Need To Know About Applications

PERHAPS THE BIGGEST questions potential mystery shoppers have are who do they sign up with, and how do they know if that company is legitimate or not. With so many scams surrounding mystery shopping, this can often be difficult to determine. If you type "mystery shopping" into an online search engine, chances are you'll find numerous sites that would love to help you out . . . for a fee.

First and foremost, you *never* have to pay for the list of mystery shopping providers. The list is available for free at the MSPA's website. This list is literally several hundred companies long, and each company included on the list has proven itself to be legitimate. Remember, as we talked about earlier, each mystery shopping provider services its own unique niche. Some may be focused on the food industry while others may focus on grocery stores and gas stations. Some may be more geographically focused on shops in the Pacific Northwest, while another only does shops in the state of Florida. Visiting the provider's website should give you some basic information about what areas they specialize in.

Not all providers will have new shops for you every day. And when new shops are posted, there may be several shoppers competing for that same shop. So to maximize the number of jobs you have to choose from and apply for, a good rule of thumb is to sign up with a minimum of 10 providers, and preferably 20 or more.

Applying with a provider can be a time-consuming process. Applying with 10-20 providers may take you the better part of a week, done in your free time. So you may want to be somewhat selective about which providers you sign up with and ensure each one you sign up with will have shops for you. Definitely look at each provider's website to get a feel for what that company specializes in. Look for providers who service niches and areas that appeal to you as a shopper.

Then also check the mystery shopper forums online to hear first hand what experiences mystery shoppers have had with specific companies. Are the companies good to work with? Do the companies pay promptly? Which companies have mystery shoppers had bad experiences with? As with anything else, take these comments with a grain of salt. One bad comment should not turn you away from a provider. However, if several shoppers seem to be having bad experiences with that company, you may want to skip over that provider for now. You can post your own specific questions on the forums and get personalized responses back on your question. So if you don't see anything posted about a specific company, don't be shy about asking for information.

There are companies that market themselves as mystery shopping providers, but in actuality they are not. These bogus companies will charge an up-front fee when you apply with them. A good rule of thumb is if a company is asking you for money, turn the other way and run. *Legitimate mystery shopping providers will not require a fee to apply.*

The Nitty Gritty Of An Application

Some applications are relatively user friendly. They require your basic contact information, including your phone number and email address. As with any other job, you will be required to provide your social security number to apply also. Then there will be some questions more specific to the job you're applying for. For instance, you may be asked if you have access to a digital camera or video camera, or to rank your top five strengths such as dependability, detail-oriented, and so forth.

Most providers will also ask for basic information about your background and physical traits, such as age, height, race, income level, and so forth. This may seem like very personal information. It is certainly more information than what is typically required (or legally allowed) with other employers. First, keep in mind that this information is not being requested as a qualification for employment. Once you have been approved as a shopper, these questions will be used to determine which shops you will be a match for. For instance, if a shop assignment requires a shopper to try on bras at Victoria's Secret, the requirement for doing the shop may be for a female shopper that is 20-45 years old. A 60-year old man would be a bad match for this type of shop. Of if a shop assignment requires you to try on a suit in a big and tall men's shop, a five foot tall woman would not be a match. Many stores requesting mystery shoppers want to make sure their mystery shopper does not appear out of character with their typical clientèle.

A typical, fairly straightforward application may take you about 10-20 minutes to complete. However, some applications are much more complex and time-consuming. These more complex applications may include a sample of your writing style through an essay question. An example essay question may be what qualities you have that would make you a good mystery shopper. Another may be why you want to be a mystery shopper. Remember, most mystery shops have some type of essay-type questions in their reports, so your ability to communicate effectively in a written format is critical. With these essay questions, the content of your answers will be critiqued just as much as your writing style, grammar, and spelling.

Other applications may have multiple choice questions that follow these same topics. For instance, you may be asked to select which of the following top three reasons are indicative of why you want to be a mystery shopper. Or you may be asked to select which five characteristics you believe are most important for a mystery shopper to have.

There are a handful of providers that ask you to complete an example shop. They will provide you with the details of the shop, and you'll be required to complete the report along with the essay-style questions based on their example.

With these applications, keep in mind the requirements of the job. For instance, top skills or traits of a mystery shopper may be the ability to meet deadlines, highly responsible, ethical, and superior writing ability. While we all want to make money doing this job, it's advisable to use the application to communicate some other non-monetary desire for doing this job as well. This may include an interest in helping companies improve their customer service or the desire to have your voice be heard by retailers.

As I mentioned, researching these companies and completing 10-20 applications can take a better the part of a week if you devote part-time hours to it. The big question that many new shoppers ask may be, "Will this be worth the effort?" That's an awful lot of time to spend applying for jobs you may not get. Well, the good news is that most providers accept a high number of their shopper applications. Of course, the answers on your applications should fall in line with what the providers are looking for in a shopper. Hopefully this book has given you some insight into that. You should also have completed your sample shops and essay questions free of errors and typos. Provided this was all done correctly, most new applications will be approved. So spend time completing the applications professionally and correctly rather than rushing through them. Then rest easy knowing your hard work on the applications should pay off.

Chapter 4

How To Avoid Scams and Identity Theft

Protect Your Social Security Number

AS YOU ARE completing online applications to work for mystery shop providers, inevitably you will pause at the section requesting your social security number. And you are justified in giving this a second thought. With identity theft prevalent in the headlines, most people are much more cautious about providing such information to anyone and especially to transmit that information via the internet.

If you have taken the time to do your research on the companies you are signing up for and if they are on the MSPA's list of legitimate shop providers, you can rest assured they are legitimate. Providers, as with any other legitimate employer, require your social security number before hiring or contracting you to work for them. They are first ensuring that you are legally available to work in the United States. Secondly, they need your social security number to report your income to the IRS at the end of the year.

Watch For Other Scams

The scary fact of the matter is that a good scam artist doesn't need your social security number to rip you off. There are certainly many companies that set themselves up to appear to be legitimate shop providers, if not to steal your social security number then to steal your money. Some shoppers have been fooled into losing hundreds and thousands of dollars.

Some of the more common scams involve companies claiming to help new shoppers get established in the industry. Who better for a predator to prey on than the people who know little about the industry? *If you learn nothing else from reading this book, know that you absolutely do not need to pay any company a dime to make money as a mystery shopper.* Some companies will offer to sell you a list of mystery shop providers for a fee. A list of legitimate mystery shop providers is available for free on the Mystery Shop Providers Association website, *www.mysteryshop. org*. There is no need to pay for a list. Further, if you get your hands on a list that includes mystery shop providers that aren't on the MSPA's list, avoid those providers. Making "a" list doesn't make the provider legitimate. Any crooked company can compile a list of crooked shop providers or scam artists. The MSPA is the only source for this list that is recognized throughout the industry.

Some companies will claim that the only way to make a decent buck as a mystery shopper is to get certified, and then they will attempt to sell you a bogus certification. The only certifications that are recognized by legitimate shop providers are those obtained through the MSPA. A discussion on certifications will be provided later in this book. However, you do not need the MSPA certifications to become a mystery shopper or to get shop assignments.

There are also other types of mystery shop scams. A popular scam is to require a mystery shopper to deposit a check into their bank account, and then immediately write a check for that same amount out of your account, without waiting for the initial check to clear. Unfortunately, the first check that the mystery shopper has deposited into their account inevitably bounces, while the check they have written out of their own account clears. The result is mystery shoppers losing thousands of dollars! Some legitimate shops will require the purchase of a small item, which will be reimbursed later. However, you should not be asked to do anything that sounds suspicious or fraudulent.

When You Are A Victim

Hopefully you will never become a victim of a scam. However, if you feel you have been approached by an illegitimate company or have fallen victim to a scam, immediately file a report with the Federal Trade Commission. When you help the FTC track and crack down on scam artists, you will help other mystery shoppers avoid being victims themselves.

If you are a victim of identity theft or a scam involving a stolen credit card number, notify your credit card company immediately. While many credit card companies have safeguards in place to protect you from liability in this type of scenario, you may still be liable for a portion of any charges to your credit card, which could result in hundreds or even thousands of dollars in lost money to you.

You should also notify all three credit bureaus as soon as you become aware you have become a victim. The bureaus are Experian, Equifax, and TransUnion. The credit bureaus will put a fraud alert on your account and can make a request that any creditors processing new credit applications in your name contact you personally by phone to verify that you are actually making the request yourself.

An Ounce Of Prevention

As the saying goes, a few steps to prevent identity theft and fraud can go a long way. There are a variety of measures you can take to limit your chances of becoming a victim. The three credit bureaus allow you to pull a credit report once a year for free. Take advantage of this, and check your report with each bureau annually. Each bureau will report slightly different information, so you want to actually check the report each bureau has for you. You specifically want to check and make sure each account open under your name is yours, and that the balances and monthly payments are approximately correct. The bureaus often have a lag time in their reporting of a few months, so don't expect your credit report to match the amount you owe today. If you notice any errors, follow the steps the credit bureaus lay out to correct them immediately.

Even if you have not been a victim of identity theft or fraud, you can request that the credit bureaus put a notice in your credit report to verify any applications for credit made under your social security number or name by verbally calling the phone number you instruct before approving a request for credit.

If you are uncomfortable providing your personal social security number online when you apply to work for mystery shop providers, you can consider setting up a business entity, such as a corporation, and running your mystery shopping business through your corporation. There are some tax and legal ramifications for doing this, so you should talk to your accountant and attorney in detail before taking this step. However, when you run your mystery shop business through your own corporation or other business entity, you can provide your entity's tax ID number rather than your personal social security number. This doesn't provide foolproof prevention for you becoming a victim of identity theft, but it does provide an extra step for crooks to go through in order to get to your personal information. Setting up a corporation or other entity is a simple process that you can do by filing paperwork at your state's Secretary of State department. There are some fees, but you may find the extra peace of mind this gives you is well worth the effort and cost.

Another step you can consider is purchasing identity theft insurance. Most major insurers are now providing this information for a small monthly fee. While the coverage varies between insurers, you will find that most identity theft insurance covers legal charges and personal losses you may incur if you become a victim of identity theft.

Similar to identity theft insurance is identity theft protection services, provided by such companies as LifeLock, Identity Guard, and TrustedID, to name a few. These companies not only provide similar coverage as identity theft insurance, but they take steps to prevent you from becoming a victim. These are turn-key services who will contact the credit bureaus on your behalf and take fraud prevention steps for you. In addition to just covering the costs of legal services, they actually have legal staff who will work to solve issues if you do become a victim. Many of them will also remove your name from junk mail lists, cutting down the number of pre-approved credit offers you receive by mail.

If identity theft is a major concern for you, research and analyze the options available to you to prevent identity theft and protect yourself in the event you do fall victim to it. Then rest easy with your decision, knowing you've taken steps to ensure your peace of mind.

Chapter 5

Potential Income
And Hidden Ways To Maximize Your Profits

YOU CAN REALISTICALLY expect to earn about $10-20 on an average mystery shop assignment. This is purely "shop pay" and does not take into account the perks of the job, such as purchase reimbursements. An average assignment takes about thirty minutes or so to complete on-site, and then an additional thirty minutes approximately to complete the report and submit your receipt if a purchase was required. So you can expect to make approximately $10-20 per hour. This does not take into account your travel time or travel expenses.

It is very important to understand that pay varies greatly per provider, per assignment, and per your location or region. Some assignments that require the use of a digital camera or that require a longer than normal amount of time to complete may pay you significantly above that amount. Some assignments pay significantly less than this, including phone assignments, where you check on customer service over the phone of places such as a restaurant or credit card company.

More Than Meets The Eye

Unlike with many other traditional part-time jobs, mystery shopping offers you a range of perks in addition to your shop pay. On a grocery store assignment, you may get a portion of your expenses reimbursed for items you already purchase on a regular basis. Picking up a grocery store assignment or two every week or even every month is a great way to help pay for your grocery bill. You can also get reimbursements for clothing, shoes, movies, meals at restaurants, and even gas for your car. Typically, the assignment will specify that you will only receive reimbursement for up to a certain amount. For instance, on a grocery store assignment, you may see a reimbursement for up to $8 of your purchases, and shop pay of $10 or $15. For a retail clothing store, you may see a reimbursement of your purchase up to $10, with shop pay of $15.

It is important for a new mystery shopper to realize that you can actually spend more money purchasing your required items than you are getting reimbursed for. In order to make the most of mystery shopping and not end up buying needless items and spending needless money, be sure to analyze each assignment before you request it. First, check the requirements of that assignment to see if a purchase is required and how much the reimbursement is. Then ask yourself if you had intended on purchasing an item that store sells anyway. Also, if possible, try to analyze how much of your purchase would not be reimbursed and would therefore be an "out of pocket" expense. However, if you had intended on buying a certain item anyway, this is a great way to get reimbursed for purchasing something you were already going to buy! For instance, a grocery store assignment or a gas station assignment may not be incredibly lucrative, but they will cover a portion of the cost of a purchase you need to make anyway.

Two Birds With One Stone

One of the biggest time-wasters with mystery shopping will be your travel time. Many mystery shoppers will not travel outside a certain radius of their house or place of daytime employment without a rather high amount of pay for the time as well as travel expense. However, don't automatically write off assignments that are a moderate distance away. Take some time to look at the other assignments posted on the job board. Often, you can fit in several mystery shopping assignments in one outing. For instance, consider doing mystery shop assignments several towns over from yours, or in one of the closer but still more rural areas near your metro area. If you cannot locate two assignments in that same city, can you find an assignment you can satisfy en route to the distant location?

Of course, you don't have to look at fitting in two or three mystery shop assignments in one outing for a distant location. If you can find several assignments near your house or place of employment, that's all the better. Anytime you accept an assignment – or before you even request the assignment, take a moment to look and see what other assignments are available nearby.

There may be assignments you want to complete, but that are located too far away to make it financially a poor decision for you to complete. Often, these assignments are in rural locations where other mystery shoppers are not keen on traveling to as well, and this results in an assignment sitting on the job boards for quite awhile. This means that the scheduler is probably willing to work with you in terms of re-structuring the pay or adding some additional travel or bonus pay to the compensation package to make the travel more worth your while. You would need to email the scheduler directly to request additional compensation for an assignment.

Take Advantage Of The Tax Code

I will preface this section by saying that you should always seek the advice of a tax professional or check the tax code on your own to determine eligibility of write-offs.

When you are employed in a typical part-time job, such as a salesperson in a retail store, you will travel to work on your own dime and then your employer will take a deduction from your paycheck for your taxes. When you are self-employed, such as you when you are a mystery shopper, you can write off various business-related expenses on your tax returns. For instance, if you earned $10,000 as a mystery shopper one year, and your business-related expenses for that year are $3,000, you would only pay taxes on $7,000. In your same "normal" job, you would have paid taxes on the full $10,000.

In addition, as a self-employed mystery shopper, you are permitted by the IRS to write off a portion of your travel expenses. The most common way for mystery shoppers to do this is by keeping track of your mileage during each mystery shopping trip you make. Simply write down your total mileage for the round trip distance of your assignment, as well as the date and location you visited in a notebook, or mileage log. At the end of the year, add up all of your mystery shopping-related mileage. Let's say your total mileage for the year is 1,000 miles. Currently, the IRS allows you to deduct $0.55 per mile. So your 1,000 miles equates to the ability to write-off $550 of mystery shopping income.

As a self-employed worker, you can also deduct any business expenses, including expenses related to your home office, office supplies, and equipment such as a computer, printer, fax machine, and digital camera.

Chapter 6

A Typical Day & Typical Jobs

DESPITE ALL OF the information in this book up to this point, you may still not have a clear understanding of what a day in the life of a mystery shopper may be like. After you have signed up to work for several providers, you can begin looking for job postings at any time.

Finding a Job

Many providers will send emails out to mystery shoppers either announcing specific jobs or announcing when their website has been updated with new jobs. So first and foremost, be sure to check your email regularly, and ideally several times per day. Keep in mind that many providers will divvy up new mystery shop assignments on a first come, first serve basis. So the more frequently you check your email, the better your likelihood of being that early bird who gets the job assignment.

Save The Date

When you sit down at your computer to search for jobs, keep your calendar or schedule in front of you. Be sure you are looking at a schedule that has all of your work and personal obligations in one spot. This way, when you look at job postings, you can quickly skip over assignments that overlap other obligations you already have in place and avoid the possibility of double booking.

Even if you are simply requesting an assignment and are waiting to hear back from the provider on if you got the job, be sure to pencil that assignment in your calendar to avoid double booking.

Using a calendar also allows you to easily see if your schedule allows for time to book two or even three assignments in one outing. It is in your best interest as a mystery shopper to make the most beneficial use of your time, so the ability to do several assignments while you are out is key to making more money as a mystery shopper.

The Requirements

Each mystery shopping assignment will have its own unique set of requirements for you to complete. Be sure to read the requirements at least the day before your assignment to make sure you understand what you are supposed to do. Some requirements specify that you call ahead before your site visit to schedule an appointment with someone or to verify the store location, and so on. So the sooner you can read through the requirements, the better.

Be sure you understand the requirements in detail. Then commit the requirements to memory. You cannot take the requirements into the store with you, so you need to memorize what you are supposed to do inside the store. A typical assignment may have you make a mental note of the time you entered the store, then note how long it takes for the salesperson to greet you. You will have to remember the salesperson's names, and details of conversations you have with the sales staff. You may also have to check the fitting rooms and restrooms for cleanliness. Some requirements specify that you try on a particular item, such as a pair of shoes or an item from a specific department. Some requirements want you to look at the display shelves to ensure they are neat and orderly, or set up in the correct fashion.

Restaurant, gas station, movie theater, and grocery store assignments will all have their own set of standard requirements, and there will be variation in the requirements from retailer to retailer and provider to provider. The important thing is to read and understand the requirements beforehand so you are able to complete the task at hand once you are at the store.

Create Your Story

With many assignments, you don't necessarily need a cover story. For instance, with a restaurant assignment or a grocery store assignment, most anyone with any traits or attributes can pull off the assignment without standing out in the crowd.

But if you are a 60 year old man doing a mystery shopping assignment at a children's clothing store or a single woman driving a two-seater sports car who needs to test drive a mini van, a cover story is probably going to be required.

First, be sure not to make your story too complicated. Think about what scenarios sound fairly plausible based on your unique circumstances. Ask yourself, why would I ever be in this store? The 60 year old man can simply act like a grandfather buying a gift for a grandchild. The single woman who arrives at the dealership to test drive a mini van can certainly say she's borrowing the car while hers is in the shop, or she can say she needs the mini van for her business. With any story that you concoct, think the details through just a little bit. A lot of salespeople will attempt to interact with you based on information you give them. So it won't be uncommon to hear a salesperson ask how old the grandkids are or how long the woman has been in the catering business.

Then, have an easy one-liner you can pull out in case your story starts getting blown to pieces. Your one-liner will be something you can standardly use to cover for any flubbing or faltering you do. You may want to say, "Oh, sorry about that. I took some allergy medicine this morning and am a little groggy." Or try, "My daughter/sister is visiting with her new baby, and I haven't been getting much sleep lately." Your one-liner will be something that you can say to buy some time while you mentally try to figure out a good way to answer the original question that got you into trouble. This rarely happens, but your one-liner will be your saving grace from getting your cover blown.

I'm Here . . . Now What?

Being in the store and trying to play it cool can be rather stressful. That little secret in your head about your mystery shopping may eat at you and make you feel like you are standing out like a sore thumb. You may feel like all the salespeople are staring holes in you. Try very hard to keep the thought in the back of your head that you are simply another shopper. If you would normally smile in response to a salesperson when they look your direction, go ahead and smile. Try to act as naturally as you normally would if you had walked into the store on your own accord.

Hopefully you made a mental to-do list based on the job assignments before you entered the store. Run through your list in your head and accomplish each task one by one. Make mental notes of the times that you are required to pay attention to, look at name tags of salespeople casually, ask to try on clothes, and so on. Before you leave the store, ensure that you have completed everything you need to and that you remember everything.

Tricks of the Trade

After you have completed a few mystery shopping assignments, you will develop your own unique method for remembering details and handling sticky situations. To get you started, I'll provide you with just a couple of helpful hints.

The details of an assignment are often the hardest to remember. For instance, in a grocery store assignment, you may be required to visit each of eight to ten departments in the store, interact with each person in the departments, and keep track of each of the clerk's names and the times you visited each department. This can be a big headache to remember. The good news is that you don't have to commit the details to memory. Most shoppers in a grocery store walk around with a pen and paper, referring to items on their list periodically and scratching things off the list as they go. Before you enter the store, make a list of each department you need to hit. It may be best to put these departments all in a column list in case someone peeks over your shoulder. This way, your list will look like a real grocery list. After you visit a department, walk away from the clerk a little ways and pretend to cross things off your list. In reality, you won't be crossing items off, but you will writing down a name, a time, and any other details you need to recall for the assignment.

This trick works in a variety of stores, such as discount stores and general stores. You can switch this technique up a bit to use in other stores. For instance, in a retail store or even a restaurant, it's very common to see people sending text messages while they shop or eat. Send yourself a text message periodically with notes about your shop. What's great about texting the notes back to yourself is that your phone will actually ring back that you received a text, so anyone paying attention to you will think you are really sending and receiving text messages.

If texting isn't your strong point, you can also use private areas of stores and restaurants to take notes with a pen and paper. For instance, on a retail store assignment, you may be required to visit both the fitting room and the bathroom to check for cleanliness and so on. Walk into the stall in these locations, and write down all of the information you need to keep track of on a small piece of paper. Then you will have a clear head to store more details as you continue the assignment.

There are literally dozens of techniques you can use such as these. Find a few that work for you, and you will make your job as a mystery shopper that much easier.

The Importance of The Report

Once your site visit is complete, you must move on to the next step, which is completing the report. The vast majority of reports you complete will be completely on-line. You will usually see some multiple choice questions as well as some detailed, essay-style questions where you need to free write your answers. There is always a deadline for completing the report, and it is typically within 12 to 24 hours of doing the site visit. Pay close attention to the report deadline, as failure to heed this requirement could result in non-payment for your time and efforts.

Some mystery shoppers mistakenly rush through the report, thinking the hard part of the assignment is over once the site visit is complete. This is a terrible thought to have. The report provides the scheduler as well as the retailer who originally ordered the mystery shop to be completed with all of the information they are looking for. The mystery shopper has essentially been the eyes and ears of the retailer, and the report is how the information you have collected on your site visit is conveyed.

The vast majority of errors or questions that come up with a report stems from too much information being provided, the question not being answered specifically as it was asked, and opinions being given instead of facts. When you are answering the questions, be sure to stick to the facts. Your report narrative should almost read like a newspaper article, keeping all of your opinions to yourself unless they are specifically asked for. It is best to provide concise answers. When too much information is given, it tends to confuse providers and the retailer by getting off topic.

Always proofread your report before you click the "submit" button online. Check for grammatical and spelling errors as well as ensuring that your responses answer the specific question asked. If the scheduler or retailer have questions about your report, your payment for the job will be delayed. So it is certainly in your best interest to do the best you can on the report.

Where's My Money?

Perhaps one of the biggest complaints mystery shoppers have about the job is slow payment. It is very common to wait four to eight weeks for a check to arrive in the mail. When you keep this time frame in mind, you will be able to relax and enjoy mystery shopping rather than spend your time getting angry that your checks are taking so long to arrive.

This time frame has quite a bit to do with the internal processing of the reports at the provider's office. Each provider has their own process, but it often involves an internal review of your report by the scheduler, followed by a review by the retailer. Once these parties have both approved the report, your check will then be processed in the accounts payable department at the provider. There are two ways typically for a payment to be sent to you, via standard postal delivery or Paypal. Some providers require you to set up a Paypal account, as they only send funds out with Paypal. You will get your money up to a week faster if you use Paypal.

If you are a mystery shopper who is looking for a somewhat steady paycheck, you need to build up a queue of paychecks by completing several jobs per week on an on-going basis. Then, once your checks start arriving, as long as you keep working, you should see a fairly steady influx of checks.

Chapter 7

Those Pesky Timed Shops

PERHAPS ONE OF the most difficult parts of a mystery shopping assignment is following the time requirements to the "T". Every assignment will have different timing requirements. Some assignments are fairly straightforward, asking you to only note the time you entered and left the store. Other assignments ask for you to make additional notes on time, such as how long the sales staff took to greet you, how long you were waiting in line or for your food order to come, or how long you were waiting in the fitting room before the salesperson came back to check on you. And then there are the real doozies, where you have to keep track of the time down to the second of various items, such as how long you stood in line, how long it took you to check out, and so on.

Keeping track of the time, especially if multiple events are being timed, while holding conversations with the sales staff and acting "normal" can be incredibly stressful, and even bordering on the impossible. To make the assignment more stressful is the looming knowledge that the details of your timed shops are often verified by video surveillance footage in the store, and if your details in the report are found to be inaccurate, you won't be paid for the assignment.

Know The Requirements

The assignments with heavy timing requirements are stressful enough without having to worry about performing the right tasks on the job site. Be sure to read through the requirements several times before you enter the store so you understand very clearly what you need to do once you are inside the store.

It often helps to visualize yourself performing each required task and do a mental walk-through of the assignment. For instance, imagine yourself noting the time you entered the store, then walking over to the display shelves to check for the right display set-up. Then imagine you are checking the bathrooms before returning to the clothing racks to pick out an item to try on. In the fitting room, skip actually trying on the clothes and instead grab a pen and paper out of your purse to write down all of the details of the site visit up to this point. Your mind is now clear to store the information you need to remember for the rest of the site visit, such as additional times. This assignment requires you to note how long you waited in the fitting room before the salesperson came to check on you, so make a note of that as well before you head out to make your purchase. You will casually glance at your wristwatch or cellphone as you get in line to check out, and then glance at the time again as you make your way to the front of the line. One more quick check of the time as you leave the store completes your visualization of the on-site visit.

Get The Right Equipment

Just as it is easier to peel a carrot with a vegetable peeler than with a knife, it's easier to keep track of the timing of the assignments when you use the right equipment for the job.

Some assignments can very easily be completed with a standard wristwatch or a cell phone. Your assignment requirements will note if you need to keep track of the time down to the second or the minute. So be sure whatever clock or watch you are using has the appropriate time display.

Other assignments are far more complicated. When you have multiple time requirements that require you to very quickly make note of back-to-back events down to the second, the only realistic way to meet the requirement is with a stop watch with a multiple event feature, such as a runner's watch that keeps track of lap times. You can pick up a fairly inexpensive runner's watch that will be able to track multiple events down to the second for you for under $30. Keep your receipt for the purchase and remember to write the purchase off as a business expense.

Avoid User Error

Having the right equipment is only half the battle. You also need to know how to use the equipment. More importantly, you have to use the equipment inconspicuously. It's not too hard to push buttons on a stop watch, but you need to be able to push the buttons on the stop watch without looking at the watch itself so you don't raise red flags to the salespeople.

Practice using the watch before your site visit. First practice pushing the buttons so you can get the watch to store the right times for you. Then practice pushing the buttons as the watch is stored in your pocket or purse.

Be sure you know exactly when to push the buttons. You don't want to be turning the timing function off when you should be starting it, and vice versa. Also be aware of what event each "lap" on the watch is recording the time for. For instance, lap one is recording the amount of time that elapsed from when you entered the store to when the salesperson greeted you, and so on. So you would push the button once when you enter the store, and then again when the salesperson approaches you.

With the right equipment for the job, you can drastically reduce the stress associated with completing these types of assignments.

Chapter 8

What's A Scheduler?

A SCHEDULER QUITE simply is the person who works for the mystery shopping providers and assigns mystery shopping assignments to mystery shoppers. There is, of course, much more to the scheduler's job duties.

The Duties Of A Scheduler

When you click on the link to "Request A Shop", your request is sent through cyberspace to the scheduler's computer. The scheduler can receive dozens of requests for a single assignment, so it is up to the scheduler to pick the best mystery shopper for the job. This decision can be based on an existing relationship with a certain mystery shopper, issues with a certain mystery shopper on a past assignment, timing constraints, location, and other factors.

In addition, the scheduler ensures that all assignments are completed on time, and that your report is accurate and complete once you have filed it. If they have any questions on the report, the scheduler is the person you will be talking to in order to clear up the questions. The scheduler then files the report with the retailer. Because of the duties relating to timing and accuracy, the scheduler has the incredible task of ensuring the mystery shopper is performing his or her job satisfactorily in order to secure future business from the retailer for their own company. Their ultimate goal is to satisfy and service the retailer.

The scheduler is also available to answer any questions you may have regarding the assignment requirements. In the event you are unable to perform the assignment, the scheduler will be required to find an alternate mystery shopper, often under the stress of a time deadline.

Why The Scheduler Should Be Your Best Friend

During your career as a mystery shopper, you will work with literally dozens of schedulers. And at some point, you will run into issues with at least one of the schedulers. These issues may result in an error on your part in completing the assignment, or it may just boil down to you having a "bad" scheduler. Emotions can run high when you are faced with the possibility of not getting paid on an assignment you worked hard on. Likewise, the scheduler has her own stresses in trying to get a satisfactory report sent to the retailer on time.

When issues arise with your scheduler, it is always best to listen with an open mind to what the scheduler is saying or asking. Avoid the temptation to get emotional and keep a professional tone to the conversation. Take an honest look at what the scheduler is saying. If necessary, make the changes the scheduler is asking and remain friendly and professional. If you honestly believe the scheduler is wrong in whatever is being asked or said, calmly explain your reason.

Mystery shoppers often get into an unnecessarily heated discussion with schedulers when issues arise. This only serves to create unnecessary issues down the road. Keep in mind that the scheduler will be the person who will be doling out assignments to you in the future – or passing your name up on assignments. While there is more than one scheduler working for each provider, the scheduler can certainly make negative comments in your profile that will impede your ability to get other assignments from that provider down the road, regardless of who the scheduler is.

Likewise, when you cultivate a relationship with a scheduler through polite and professional interactions, as well as helping the scheduler out with assignments others don't want to do, the scheduler will remember your name down the line when she is handing out the plum assignments.

Nurturing Your Relationship

As with any professional relationship, there are things you can do to nurture and promote a healthy working relationship with your schedulers.

- Remember that schedulers are busy people. You want to get to know them, but do not call them out of the blue and try to chat them up about new shops they having coming down the line soon. This may backfire on you, and you may soon get a reputation for being a nuisance.
- When your scheduler calls you about your report, respond to them as professionally, positively, and accurately as you can. Give them the impression that you appreciate their efforts on working with you on the report, and follow all of their instructions to the tee. They will remember you as someone they enjoy working with.
- A scheduler may also contact you personally about an assignment they are having difficulty placing. Often this will be a dud of a job that other mystery shoppers are passing over for a reason. It may seem like more effort or time than the pay is worth. However, you may want to consider doing this shop to promote yourself to the scheduler, and to help your name stick out to the scheduler for future assignments. Remember, the scheduler needs to get this assignment done to satisfy their client, and helping them out is a great way to get the scheduler to remember you. It's the karma of mystery shopping – help them out, and good things will come back to you.

A good relationship will take time to develop, but when you follow these general guidelines, you will be well on your way to becoming a favorite mystery shopper with your scheduler!

Chapter 9

Busted! How To Handle Being Revealed As A Mystery Shopper – And How To Avoid It

THE THOUGHT OF being revealed as a mystery shopper strikes fear in the hearts of mystery shoppers everywhere. You are "revealed" when store staff are tipped off that you are a mystery shopper. They may make a comment to you while you are in the store, or you may hear about your revealed status later from your scheduler.

If It Happens To You

If the store's staff makes a comment to you about you being a mystery shopper, you can certainly deny their comments if you feel their suspicions are unjustified. You can even go so far as to play dumb about the possibility of mystery shopping even being "real." However, if you feel that you have legitimately made a mistake that has tipped the store's staff about your identity, it's best to exit the store as fast as you can. Even then, however, never admit openly that you are in fact a mystery shopper. Once you return home, notify your scheduler immediately that you believe you were revealed.

If the scheduler notifies you after you have completed the site visit that the store's staff has identified you as a mystery shopper, most likely your efforts will be void and you will not be paid for the job.

In most cases, being identified will not necessarily go on your record as a bad mark unless you have legitimately made an error that resulted in you being revealed. Typically, you will just not be permitted to complete an assignment at that location again in the future.

How It Happens

Perhaps one of the most common ways a mystery shopper is revealed is by mystery shopping at the same location too frequently. A store's staff may be have been suspicious of you on your last visit and your appearance may have raised red flags to them this time.

Or perhaps you had a lengthy conversation with the store's staff about something that stood out to them. For whatever reason, your comment about your goldfish dying or your child learning to tie his shoes stuck out in the salesperson's head. When you made a note about that conversation in your report, the details likely worked their way back to the salesperson, who could then recognize your face as a mystery shopper on your return visit.

Or it may be something more overt that occurs during the visit. Perhaps the salesperson overheard you on a cell phone conversation saying you have to complete your job at the store. You may have brought a child with your on the assignment who blew your cover. Or maybe your technique at digging for information, such as a name from a salesperson who wasn't wearing a name tag, seemed suspicious. Any number of things can happen during your site visit that make identify you as a mystery shopper, or that may make you seem suspicious.

Preventing The Bust

Since so many things can happen to reveal your identity as a mystery shopper, there is no one single thing you can do to prevent being busted. However, there are some general steps you can take to limit the likelihood of being busted.

First, avoid shopping at the same location repeatedly. A good rule of thumb is not to do the same assignment twice within a six month period. The exception to this rule, however, is if the assignment is at a location you already frequent, such as your neighborhood gas station or grocery store.

With any assignment, try to keep your conversations with the salespeople fairly generic. While you likely will need to create a good cover story during some of your assignments, avoid going into too much detail with your story. Also avoid making you cover story so outlandish and unbelievable that you will stand out and be remembered next time you visit the store. If you are normally a "people person" who can develop relationships in just a few minutes of meeting a person, you may need to tone down this skill and become more of a wallflower while you are mystery shopping. The bottom line is that you don't want the salesperson to remember you.

Also, avoid doing anything that will make you look suspicious to the salespeople. This could be staring at the display shelves for too long, pulling out your assignment instructions, walking systematically from aisle to aisle without pretending to browse the merchandise, or looking at your watch and then blatantly writing the time down on a piece of paper. Above all else, don't just pretend to be a normal shopper, but actually BE a normal shopper. Put yourself in the actual mindset that you walked into the store to try on a pair of shoes or to buy some groceries. Perhaps something on the shelf caught your eye and you meander over there. Don't make a straight line from the front door to the display shelves in the back without spending some time actually looking at the merchandise, as any other shopper would do.

If you use commonsense when you are at a job site and actually get into the mindset that you are shopping (or dining, or whatever activity most people that visit the location do), you will blend into the crowd. Your goal is to blend in and not be remembered.

Chapter 10

How To Avoid Burnout

MYSTERY SHOPPING CAN be an incredibly rewarding job. While the pay isn't necessarily top dollar, the hours are flexible, you can write off a number of expenses you can't write off on a normal job, and you can still make more on most days than you can for flipping burgers or working retail.

Yet, as with most jobs, many mystery shoppers eventually develop the feeling that the fun has disappeared from the job or that the pay just isn't worth the effort. When you mystery shop from day to day, it is often easy to lose sight of the many advantages mystery shopping has over other part-time jobs. There are some steps you can take to avoid getting burned out with mystery shopping.

Do What Makes You Happy

As you get more experienced with mystery shopping, you may branch out a little bit and experiment with different types of assignments. Mystery shopping touches so many industries, from banking, entertainment, retail, food, gas, and others. With so many options to choose from, you most certainly will find a certain type of assignment you prefer to do. Mystery shoppers on a rigid diet or with special dietary needs may not be the best fit for restaurant assignments. Bookworms may not get much satisfaction out of doing movie trailer checks at movie theaters.

There is almost certainly a type of assignment that you prefer to work on, and possibly a handful of providers that you prefer to work with over others. The beauty of mystery shopping is that you can choose which assignments you want to take and which providers you want to work with. If you have a bad experience, there is absolutely no need to repeat it. You can't say that about a bad day on any other type of job!

Check The Compensation

Nothing turns a mystery shopper off faster than feeling under-appreciated and underpaid for their efforts. Before you request an assignment, be sure you have fully analyzed the assignment and the compensation. A $10 shop pay on a report with sixty essay questions or with numerous details is likely one that will leave you feeling bitter and resentful. Also check the travel time, travel expense, and required purchase to ensure you won't be in the red on the assignment. If the assignment isn't making you money or compensating you for purchases you already planned to make, skip over it.

Timing Is Everything

The flexibility of mystery shopping is often one of the most appealing attributes of the job. The job is as well-suited for night-shift employees as it is for soccer moms, and is just as ideal for college students as it is for retired seniors. With so many assignments to choose from with such varying time requirements, there is no reason that completing an assignment on time should be stressful. Before you sign up for an assignment, be sure you will have enough time to complete it. You can certainly pick up an assignment on your lunch break from your regular job, or on the way home from work in the evening, but be sure you won't be too stressed.

Also keep in mind that there are two parts to the assignment. The first is the site visit, and the second is completing the report. Ensure that you allow yourself enough time to do the report in the evening to avoid any last minute rushes. If accepting the assignment will put you in a time pickle, skip over that assignment and pick up the next one that comes along.

If You Do Get Burned Out

Burn out can – and does – happen to the best mystery shoppers. You can be cruising along with your mystery shopping gig one day, completing assignments, developing relationships with schedulers, and getting regular paychecks. Then suddenly one day it hits and you become dissatisfied with mystery shopping. Perhaps you feel the pay isn't worth your efforts or the work is too complicated. Or perhaps you've been taking on too many assignments and simply need to take a break.

If you feel like taking a break from mystery shopping, by all means do so! Unlike most jobs, with mystery shopping you can simply stop requesting assignments for a few days, for a week, or even for several months. There is absolutely no need to feel guilty about not working, because there are always other mystery shoppers who can pick up the assignments. Then when you've had a sufficient break and are ready to start mystery shopping again, you simply start requesting assignments again. It's as simple as that. You will be able to step right back into the job where you left off.

If you do get burned out, it's important to keep in mind the benefits of the job, such as the ability to set your own hours, select your own assignments, and write off business-related expenses. There are a large number of part-time jobs out there that you can do that may provide more stable paychecks, but they won't provide you these additional benefits. And these are the benefits that likely brought you to mystery shopping in the first place.

www.ingramcontent.com/pod-product-compliance
Lightning Source LLC
Chambersburg PA
CBHW021930170526
45157CB00005B/2268